STUDIES IN THE BOOK OF JOSHUA: THE COVENANTS IN ACTION

By: Ariel Berkowitz

Distributed by:

Shoreshim Publishing

TIMELESS TORAH TRUTHS
דברי אמת התורה לעולם ועד

Shoreshim Publishing
71040 Memphis Ridge Rd.
Richmond, Michigan 48062
Phone: 586-588-0193
Email: print@shoreshimtri.com
www.shoreshimtri.com

STUDIES IN THE BOOK OF JOSHUA: THE COVENANTS IN ACTION

Ariel Berkowitz

ISBN: 978-0-9904378-6-4

Shoreshim Publishing. 68786 S. Main St. Richmond, MI 48062-1545 USA
Website: www.shoreshimtri.com
E-mail: print@shoreshimtri.com

The author is a part-time instructor with TorahResource Institute, as well as a full-time teacher with Torah Resources International. Questions about the material are welcome. Please address them to Ariel at ad.tri@mac.com.

The Cover: The cover map is from the Satellite Bible Atlas (SBA) produced by Dr. William Schlegel, professor at "IBEX," the Israeli Campus of The Master's University. This map on the cover is a diagram of Joshua's northern campaign in Canaan as he drew the coalition of Canaanite armies to battle at the Waters of Merom in Joshua 11.

Cover

The cover map is from the Satellite Bible Atlas (SBA) produced by Dr. William Schlegel, a professor at "IBEX," the Israeli Campus of The Master's University. To us this picture depicts some of the main themes of the *Book of Joshua*. This map shows Joshua's northern campaign in Canaan as he drew the coalition of Canaanite armies to battle at the Waters of Merom. This is the largest battle recorded in Joshua. The blue lines indicate the directions from which the various Canaanite armies came to meet the challenge of Joshua and his army. Joshua was greatly outnumbered and suffering from inferior military technology. However, those problems would not deter Joshua from engaging this huge force of Canaanites because, as we are told throughout the book, God would be the One who would fight for Israel! It is God who told Joshua how to defeat the Canaanites. It is God who caused the great victory that Joshua won that day. All Joshua had to do was to listen to his Commander–in-Chief that he met in chapter 5 and the victory was his.

Preface

I would like to emphasize a few items that are important for the reader to understand before using this booklet. First, please note that this is a self-study booklet. Among other things, this means that it is not intended to be a thorough exegesis of the *Book of Joshua*. Many passages are not included and various concepts are not covered. We have tried to keep footnotes to a minimum. For the most part, when we have quoted someone, it is found in a grey box with the appropriate information included. However, we have provided a bibliography of the main sources that we used in studying Joshua.

Second, the questions are based on the text of the New American Standard Bible. However, some of our quotations, especially memory verses, are based on our translation from the original Hebrew.

Next, we would like to express our gratitude to the following sources for permission to use visual aids:

1. Maps: Unless stated, we made our own maps using the Atlas resource provided by Accordance, an electronic Bible study program produced by OakTree Software (https://www.accordancebible.com/).

2. Chapter 2:

   The "Aerial view of Tell Jericho," under the heading "The Mission of the Spies," is from www.BiblePlaces.com, a website owned and produced by Todd Bolen, a friend and former instructor. This is a premier site for photographs of places in Israel and in the greater Mediterranean world that are pertinent to the Scriptures. Dr. Bolen is currently Associate Professor of Biblical Studies at The Master's University.

3.   Chapter 3:

  a.   "Tell Jericho, looking west," under the heading "Pictures of Jericho Archaeology," is also courtesy of BiblePlaces.com.

  b.   "The Walls of Jericho" on the same page is from Gene Fackler, Associates for Biblical Research. www.BibleArchaeology.org.

  c.   The two pictures of the Judean Wilderness under the heading, "The Southern Campaign" are courtesy of BiblePlaces.com.

  d.   The picture of Gibeon, under the heading "The Southern Campaign," is courtesy of BiblePlaces.com.

  e.   The two maps under the heading of "The Northern Campaign" are courtesy of our friend and colleague, William Schlegel in his work entitled, The Satellite Bible Atlas. Dr. Schlegel is the director of the Israeli campus of The Master's University, called by the acronym, IBEX (Israel Bible Extension Program.) I teach there on a part-time basis.

  f.   Picture of Tell Hazor, just before the heading, "Down with the Anakim! — Joshua Chapters 11:21-23 — courtesy of BiblePlaces.com

  g.   The "Regional Schematic Map," under the "Summary," is also courtesy of Bill Schlegel from The Satellite Bible Atlas.

  h.   In Chapter 6, the picture of Mounts Gerizim and Ebal are also courtesy of Bibleplaces.com

We have other important items that we need to include in this Preface. The student might notice that we use the word "Torah" instead of the usual term, "Law." That is purposeful and quite important. The Bible uses the word Torah in the Hebrew text. "Torah" is a word that means "teaching" or "instruction." It does not mean "law." Moreover, the Book of the Torah (*sefer haTorah*, ספר התורה) is a title that the Bible itself gives to the Five Books of Moses. It is a phrase also found at least twice in the *Book of Joshua* (1:8 and 8:34).

Torah is a book where God teaches His covenant people how to live as His covenant people. Referring to this part of the Bible as "The Law" is, in our opinion, not only distracting, but also unfortunate. For a more complete treatment on the nature of the Torah, please see our work entitled, *Torah Rediscovered*. Simply order it from TorahResource.com.

Finally, we would like to thank the following for help in producing this booklet:

Gary Springer of TorahResource for the inspiration and inception of this study booklet.

D'vorah Berkowitz, my wife, for editing and encouragement

Diane Ruth Kulp for proofreading, layout, and design.

Ya'el Kresefsky for proofreading

William Schlegel: Cover Map

Rachel Berkowitz: Cover design

The Staff of TorahResource Institute: Technical help

May the Holy One of Israel, the God of Covenants, truly bless you as you embark on this study of the *Book of Joshua*. If there are any questions, please feel free to contact us at: ad.tri@mac.com.

Objective

S TUDIES IN THE BOOK OF JOSHUA: THE COVENANTS IN ACTION is a self-study on the biblical *Book of Joshua*. It is designed for the student to think through the entire *Book of Joshua* at his/her own pace. The plan is to explore the *Book of Joshua* section by section by reading the biblical text and answering the questions by filling in the blanks that we have provided. Along the way, there are key passages to memorize, maps to peruse, and pictures that will help to elucidate the passage under investigation.

We have several goals in mind in this study. First, we hope to facilitate the earnest Bible student to become more familiar with the contents and flow of thought in the *Book of Joshua*. Second, we desire to help the student to see how the *Book of Joshua* shows the way in which God's covenants with Israel work together to define and direct God's people as a people. Finally, we want to help the student to gain a better understanding of the Holy One as a God who is in covenant relationship with His covenant community.

CHAPTER ONE

Background Information

Details about the Person of Joshua

1. Joshua's name is cited 27x in the Torah.

2. The first mentioning of Joshua's name is in Exodus 17:8-13. In what capacity is Joshua functioning in this passage?

    _____

    _____

3. According to Exodus 24:13, Joshua served as

    _____

4. Numbers 13 describes the role Joshua and _____ played in attempting to persuade the Israelites to_____. What were some of the main arguments that they used against those who disagreed? Read 13:30; 14:6-9.

    _____

    _____

    _____

5. What did Moshe do to Joshua in Numbers 13:16?

    _____

    What is (are) the possible difference (s) between the two names?___

    Why do you think Moshe did this?

    _____

    _____

6. What did Moshe ask the Lord in Numbers 27:15-17 and why did he ask this?

    _____

    _____

    _____

7. How did God answer Moshe's request in Numbers 27:18-23?

    _____

    _____

8. What are some of the things Moshe did to indicate that leadership was being transferred to Joshua? Try to ascertain the possible reasons for each step in the process.

    a. 27:18 – _____

        Why? _____

    b. 27:19 – _____

        Why? _____

    c. 27:20 – _____

        Why? _____

    d. 27:21 – _____

        Why? _____

    e. 27:22-23 – _____

        Why? _____

9. Right after Moshe went to be with the Lord, we are told in Deuteronomy 34:9 that Joshua received _____.

    For what reason do you think this happened?

    _____

    What was the reaction of the Israelites to this in 34:9?

    _____

    _____

10. What does the Lord repeat to Joshua in the following verses, and why do you think there is such a repetition?

    Deuteronomy 31:4, 7, 23   Joshua 1:6, 9, 18; 10:25

    _____

    Why?

    _____

    _____

11. Read through the *Book of Joshua* and observe how many times Moshe is mentioned in this book. For what purpose or purposes do you think he is so frequently mentioned?

    _____

    _____

    _____

12. What interesting title does Moshe and Joshua have in common, and what are the circumstances that surround the Lord pronouncing that title upon them? See Deuteronomy 34:5 and Joshua 24:29

    The Title: _____

    The Circumstances: _____

    _____

13. At what age did Joshua die? Joshua 24:29 _____

Things One Should Know before Studying Joshua

Before one begins a study of the *Book of Joshua*, there are certain "pre-requisites" that are necessary in order to facilitate his/her understanding of and accurate interpretation of the text. We do not consider these matters to be secondary to our study. Rather, we think that knowing them is a must for any earnest Bible student.

1. The Torah

    The Pentateuch provides the background, both historically and theologically, for the *Book of Joshua*.

    a.   God promised to give Abraham and his descendants a land of their own (Gen 12:7; 13:14-17; 15:7; et al.). The fulfillment of that promise is the primary focus of the *Book of Joshua*.

    b.   The person and work of Moshe are among the most prominent features in Joshua. Many parallels are intentionally drawn between the lives of Moshe and Joshua.

    c.   The *Book of Joshua* is closely related to the Book of Deuteronomy; even the language is sometimes similar.

    d.   Genesis and Deuteronomy provide respectively the prologue and the conclusion for Exodus, Leviticus, and Numbers, where the focus is on the Torah/Instruction and the covenant.

2.   The Concept and Role of Covenant

    a.   The Definition of Covenant

    The word "covenant" can be defined as a legally binding relationship between two or more people. Covenants were common in the ancient Near East; being in use long before the Bible was written. We can understand biblical covenants by studying those Ancient Near Eastern covenants. Moreover, we see that God used the covenant format in which to communicate His covenants to both Abraham and Moshe.

    b.   The Importance of the Abraham Covenant in Joshua

    It is in God's covenantal promises to Abraham where we find that the children of Abraham through Jacob have a legal and divine right to ownership of the Promised Land.

    In the *Book of Joshua*, we see two things happening that have to do with the covenant to Abraham. First, we see Israel, the covenantal descendants of Abraham, finally claiming their right to the Land. Second, we see Israel being used by God as an instrument of justice to the ungodly Canaanites/Amorites as they took the Land. This is in fulfillment of the prediction God made to Abraham when the Lord ratified that covenant in Genesis 15. The Lord said, in Genesis 15:16, that after serving as slaves in Egypt for a period of time, God would bring them out of Egypt and lead them to the Land of Promise. He said to Abraham, "in the fourth generation they [Abraham's descendants] will return here [to Canaan], for the iniquity of the Amorite is not yet complete." This implies that Israel would be the tool of God's justice against the Amorites (also called Canaanites).

c.   The Importance of the Mosaic Covenant in Joshua

When the Holy One brought the descendants of Abraham out of slavery in Egypt, He led them to Mount Sinai on their way home to the Land. There, He made another covenant with them. It was designed to complement the covenant with Abraham. Whereas in the Abrahamic Covenant the Israelites received the divine promise of the Land, in the Covenant of Mount Sinai they received instructions about how to live in the Land. Or, in other words, one might say the Mount Sinai covenant (The Torah) is a description of what it is like to live as God's covenant people.

If Israel were to live according to those instructions they would experience the blessings of fruitfulness in the Land and the enjoyment of living in the Land. The *Book of Joshua* demonstrates that when Israel was faithful to those instructions, Israel was successful in taking the Land. However, the sequel to Joshua, the Book of Judges, shows what happens when God's covenant people were not faithful to the covenant. They would experience the covenant problems which the covenant itself delineates in Deuteronomy chapters 27-29.

We should note that Israel's historical unfaithfulness to this covenant does not mean an end to the covenant. On the contrary, Israel historically has experienced all of the problems that were *promised* in the covenant as is written in Deuteronomy 27-30. Thus, Israel's centuries-old problems provide proof that God has still kept the covenant and has treated Israel as if she is still a covenant partner.

3.   The Nature of Biblical War

In the Torah, God instructs Israel how to conduct herself during times of war. This is clear from Deuteronomy 20. The *Book of Joshua* is a living example of the covenant people practicing that covenantal instruction about conducting warfare.

In addition, as we stated above, according to Genesis 15, God would use Israel as a tool of His judgment against the unbelieving and sinful Canaanites / Amorites. This would involve war. In like manner, years later God would use the armies of the nations that surround Israel as similar tools of discipline for Israel when Israel would be unfaithful to the covenant.

In Deuteronomy 7:2 we read, "and when the Lord your God delivers them [the nations in the land of Canaan] before you and you defeat them, then you shall utterly destroy them. You shall make no covenant with them and show no favor to them." The words that are translated "utterly destroy" represent the Hebrew word "*charam*, חרם." As part of the charam, they were instructed to take no spoil of war from the people whom they were instructed to destroy. The idea is that Israel was to have no mercy. For centuries, the Holy One had been making Himself known to the inhabitants of Canaan, yet they persisted in doing their detestable religious practices as they propagated allegiance to false gods. However, it is clear from Joshua that whoever gave their allegiance to the God of Israel would be spared, such as we shall see with Rahav. The people were to be destroyed and wherever the Lord commanded it, Israel was to take no spoils of war. That is the nature of the charam.

> "Since the warfare was commanded by the Lord and represented his judgment on the Canaanites, the Israelites were on a divine mission with the Lord as their commander. Since it was His war, not theirs, and He was the victor, the spoil belonged to Him... The practice of burning everything after the defeat of a city thus had an element of health connected to it."
>
> — IVP *Old Testament Background Commentary*, 178.

In addition to all of that, when we explore the battles in the *Book of Joshua*, it soon becomes evident at that God is the One who fights for Israel. For this reason, Israel can exclude certain people (eg. Deuteronomy 20) — the size of the army is not an issue.

4. Biblical Geography

Without question, it is extremely difficult to work one's way through the *Book of Joshua* without a basic knowledge of biblical geography. This is true on several levels. A knowledge of biblical geography...

a. Helps us to understand Joshua's war priorities,

It is true that Joshua planned his strategy based on the directions of his Commander in Chief, the Lord God of Israel. Yet, on a human level, Joshua planned his battles based on the knowledge he had about the lay of the land, its physical features, and the main geographic regions of the Land. His knowledge of the geography aided him greatly in planning his wars.

b. Helps us to understand the route of armies,

Why did the Amorites attempt to escape from the pursuing Israelites by fleeing down the Beit Horon Descent? Why did the Canaanites think that they could use chariots at the battle of Merom? These and other questions can best be answered when we know the geography of the Land of Israel.

c. Helps to make sense of the text.

What does it mean that the waters of the Jordan were stopped as far as Adam? Where is Adam? Why did the Lord place the cities of Refuge in the locations we see in Joshua 20? Why did the Lord choose Mount Ebal and Mount Gerizim as the place for the nation to gather to renew the covenant? The answer to these questions — and more questions like them — is found only by having a good working knowledge of the geography of the Land and being familiar with maps of the Land.

5. Archaeology

The *Book of Joshua* has been the subject of many liberal attacks. Many scholars are asserting either that the events recorded within the book did not take place or that they did not take place when the book says that they should have taken place. Archaeology is the answer to some of these objections. Since most of us are not trained archaeologists, we are at the mercy of those scholars who are. Unfortunately the voice of skeptical scholarship rings very loud so that even those who attempt to uphold the inerrancy of the Scriptures sometimes fall prey to the conclusion of the those who doubt.

Fortunately there is help and hope! Organizations such as the *Associates for Biblical Research* have done very significant work in the field to provide scholarly rebuttals to those who doubt the veracity of the historical record in the *Book of Joshua*. Bible students should be encouraged to subscribe to such magazines as *Bible and Spade* where, for example, one can read the truth about excavations at Jericho, Ai, and other places.

The Theology of Joshua

Although Joshua is a book that concerns itself largely with historical events, nevertheless, it is also replete with significant theology.

1. Jewish thinkers place Joshua among the "Prophets."

    Jewish thinkers place Joshua in the "Prophets" section of the Tanakh, rather than merely referring to it as history. It is history, but it is history from God's perspective. It is God's viewpoint on what happened. Hence, by studying it we can and do learn much about God and His sovereign role in human events.

2. God relates with His people through Covenant.

    We have already seen that knowing of the concept of covenant is essential to a proper understanding of Joshua. We will only add here that when we do study covenant, we catch a glimpse of God as a covenant-making God, and see that He relates with His people through covenant relationship.

3. God is a holy God.

    Why is it that God used the Israelites as an arm of His justice by inflicting punishment on the Canaanites? The answer is that the God of the *Book of Joshua* is a holy God. He is separate from the gods of the nations. Moreover, He has also instructed His people to live lives separate from that of the nations, that they should be holy.

4. God is a gracious God.

    When people think of the *Book of Joshua*, all too often they focus on what they say is the bloodthirsty God who directed all of the battles. When they do so, they lose sight of the fact that this same God is also a God of grace, love, and mercy. People forget that God was continually revealing Himself to the Canaanites in many different ways over the course of centuries, if not millennia. They simply rejected what they learned about the God of Israel.

    Moreover, let us not forget Rahav and the mercy shown to her when she accepted that revelation and knowledge of the true God and placed her lot with the people of God rather than clinging to her own people's religious heritage. It is this same Rahav of whom the Book of Hebrews says, "By faith Rahav the harlot did not perish along with those who were disobedient, after she had welcomed the spies in peace" (Hebrews 11:31).

5. God is a Sovereign God

    The *Book of Joshua* is full of human events. Yet, it is unmistakable that there is a sovereign God Who is behind the whole affair. As Francis Schaeffer would state it, "He is the God Who is there" and "He is there and not silent." It was

God who caused the Canaanites to hear of His astonishing actions with the Israelites, encouraging the Israelites as they began their wars. It was God who brought the kings of the Amorites together to fight against the Israelites at Gibeon, thereby causing Joshua to capture the entire southern part of Canaan. And, it was God who directed Joshua to hamstring the horses of the Canaanites at Merom, knowing full well that it would cause victory to rest with the technically inferior Israelites forces.

In short, to study the *Book of Joshua* is not only to catch a little glimpse of human history, but also to catch an even greater insight into the Sovereign God who is at the heart of human history and Who, in fact, directs human history.

Outlines

The *Book of Joshua* is relatively easy to think through. It is well organized and flows very smoothly from one section to another, from one event to another. It is in that light that we present the following outline. It is ours with the understanding that the more one becomes familiar with a book of the Bible the more one is able put forth his/her own outline — which is what we hope every student will do!

The foregoing was our outline to the *Book of Joshua*. We are using a different outline as we use this study booklet. We are emphasizing the concept of covenant in this booklet. Hence, here is how this booklet is organized:

Preface

Chapter 1:   Introduction

Chapter 2:   Covenant Preparations — Joshua Chapters 1-5

Chapter 3:   The Conquest: Claiming the Covenant Inheritance – Part 1 — Joshua Chapters 6-9

Chapter 4:   The Conquest: Claiming the Covenant Inheritance – Part 2 – Joshua Chapters 10-12

Chapter 5:   Finally: The Covenant Inheritance! — Joshua Chapters 13-21

Chapter 6:   The Finale: Living the Covenant — Joshua Chapters 22-24

It is time now to march with Joshua throughout the Land and to see the mighty and sovereign Hand of the Holy One continually at work accomplishing His purposes in human history. Have fun studying!

CHAPTER TWO

Covenant Preparations

Joshua Chapters 1-5

This chapter focuses on the preparations that were necessary before Israel could take the Land. Some of these preparations involved specific covenant activities, but there is more. Let us explore the different kinds of preparations that Joshua led Israel through before the battles begin in Joshua chapter 6.

Re-commissioning of Joshua — Joshua Chapter 1

Chapter 1 of Joshua focuses on God preparing the leader to lead the covenant people into the Land. In essence, it is a re-commissioning of Joshua, now that Moshe is gone.

> ### Memory Verse
>
> **Joshua 1:7** "Only be strong and very courageous; be careful to do according to all the Torah which Moshe My servant commanded you; do not turn from it to the right or to the left, so that you may have success wherever you go."

God Describes Joshua 1:1

1. How does the text refer to Joshua in 1:1?

   _____

   Why is it important for us to know that piece of information?

   _____

   _____

2. There are at least two possible Hebrew ways to speak of a servant: *'eved,*
    עבד and *misheret,* משרת. Joshua 1:1 uses the word *misheret.*

    Use a Hebrew lexicon or other appropriate source to see if there might be any
    difference between the two terms. Note any possible difference in the space below.

God Exhorts Joshua

3. In this re-commissioning, the Lord exhorted Joshua to do certain things.
    What are the things the Lord urged Joshua to do?

    a.   1:6; 1:7; 1:9 _____

    _____

    b.   1:7 _____

    Notes:

    — The Hebrew term behind the word "law" in 1:7-8 in most English
    translations is the word "*torah,* תורה."

    — The Hebrew term behind the word "success" ("you may have success",
    1:7-8) translations is a word for "wisdom" or "prudence," *shakal,* שקל.

    _____

4. What is the key to Joshua's success, according to 1:8?

    _____

    _____

5. What does it mean to "meditate" on God's Torah?

    _____

    _____

    How would this have helped Joshua?

    _____

    _____

God's Promises to Joshua

6. What things does God promise to Joshua if Joshua followed His exhortations? 1:5, 9

   _____

   _____

7. Even though we are not called to do as Joshua was called to do, nevertheless, in the space below list some of the ways that we can apply God's instructions to our everyday lives?

The Covenant Community

8. What is it that Joshua instructs the tribes of Reuben, Gad, and the half-tribe of Manasseh to do according to 1:12-15?

   _____

   _____

9. Why did Joshua have to give them special instructions?

   _____

10. Why was it important that they would do what Joshua was telling them?

    _____

    _____

11. What does this teach us about how the covenant community functions with each other?

_____

_____

12. What was the response of these tribes to Joshua's instructions in 1:16-18?

_____

13. Why was it important that they demonstrated such co-operation?

_____

_____

The Mission of the Spies — Joshua Chapter 2

After re-commissioning Joshua in Chapter 1, Chapter 2 focuses on the first steps toward the actual conquest.

1. What is the first military action Joshua, the general, decided to take in preparation for the conquest? 2:1

_____

_____

Why do you think this was necessary?

_____

_____

Note: there is a difference between the Hebrew words translated "spies" in Joshua 2:1 and Numbers 13:2.

Joshua 2:1 — meragglim, מרגלים (a noun) from the word for foot, *regel* (רגל). Hence, this word stresses the idea of going on foot to check out the land and gather information: "to spy."

Numbers 13:2 —yaturu, יתורו, from the verb *tur,* תור which can mean "to spy," but which also stresses the idea of discovering or exploring. In Modern Hebrew, it is the common word for a "tourist."

2. To what geographical location were the spies told to go first to gather information? 2:2 _____

3. Where specifically did they end up in this town?

    _____

    Note: This woman's occupation is often rendered as "harlot." However, there is some good evidence that the Hebrew word could easily be rendered "innkeeper."[1]

4. Strategically speaking why was this an important place for spies to be? _____

    _____

5. Notice on the map below:

    a. The location of Jericho

    b. The three roads (pathways) that led from Jericho west into the central mountains of Canaan. The main population centers were in the central mountains because

        • There is a sufficient supply of water

        • There is sufficient land to farm for food

        • There is relatively adequate protection from hostiles

        • The mountain ridges and small plateaus provide adequate communication and travel links

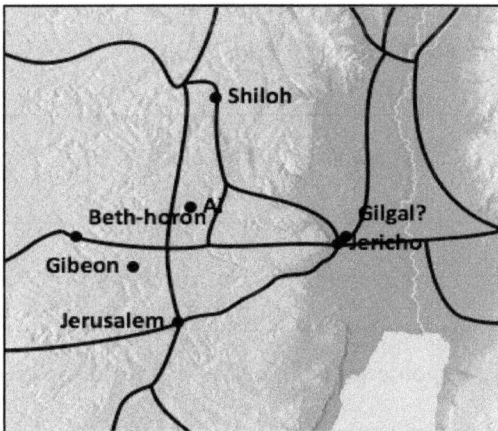

[1] Anthony J. Frendo, "Was Rahab Really a Harlot?" *Biblical Archaeology Review* 39:5, September/October 2013.

Tell Jericho, looking west.
Note how small ancient Jericho was!
The spies hid in the hills behind the tell.

6.   What did Rahav tell the spies which was important for them to know? (2:9-11)

_____

_____

7.   Why was this information important for the spies to know?

_____

_____

_____

8.   What did Rahav request of the spies? 2:13-14

_____

9.   How did Israel handle this request? 2:17-21 and 6:22-25

_____

_____

_____

10. What was Israel's response to the information that Rahav gave to the spies? 2:24

_____

_____

11. How can we reconcile Israel's treatment of, and relationship to, the Canaanite Rahav with the instructions God gave Israel in Deuteronomy 7:1-6?

_____

_____

_____

_____

12. What can Rahav's statements tell us about the covenant-keeping God?

_____

_____

_____

_____

13. Here are some possible purposes for the story about the spies

   a. It gives an example of an unbelieving Canaanite who joined up with Israel. (2:6, 17, 22–25) — An exception to the *charam*

   b. It gives an example of Israel's reputation.

      • How God was "fighting" for them? (2:9)

      _____

      _____

   c. It shows a continuation of the Messianic ancestral line.

      • Matthew 1:5 says that Rahav was part of Yeshua's ancestors.

   d. It gives an example of a woman of faith. - Hebrews 11:31

   e. Can you think of any other purpose this chapter might serve?

      _____

      _____

      _____

      _____

Crossing the Jordan — Joshua Chapters 3-4

Armed with great encouragement as a result of the report from the spies, Joshua now leads the Israelites to cross the Jordan and enter into their inheritance. Let us explore some of the fascinating details of this event.

1. According to 3:7, what is one purpose that the crossing event served for Joshua himself?

    _____

    _____

2. According to 3:10, what is one purpose that the crossing event served for the people of Israel?

    _____

    _____

A Possible Picture

We want to present a possible message that the text might be presenting, but which might be somewhat hidden under the surface. We present this information only for the student's consideration. Yet, we feel confident enough about its content to present it here. Our interpretation is based on the meaning of key Hebrew terms involved in the crossing event. Those words are:

Jordan • Adam • Joshua • The Ark of the Covenant

We shall examine each word one at a time, then put the picture together. Please bear in mind that what we are presenting is only a *suggestion*. Yet, it makes sense and could have been how the ancient Hebrew-speaking Israelites might have seen the crossing from their perspective.

The Jordan River and Adam

The Hebrew word Jordan (*yarden*, ירדן) might be associated with two words: *yarah* (ירה) and *dan* (דן). "*Yar*" is from the Hebrew word which means, "to go down" (*yarad,* ירד). "*Dan*" is a word that means "judgment."

1. What did God promise would happen when the priests brought the Ark of the Covenant into the Jordan to begin the crossing? (3:13)

    _____

_____

_____

_____

2. At what geographic location would the waters stop? (3:16)

_____

Why do you think the text might be informing us that the waters will stop at a place called "Adam"?

_____

_____

3. Let us put this part of the picture together:

   • The judgment flowing down from Adam will be stopped!

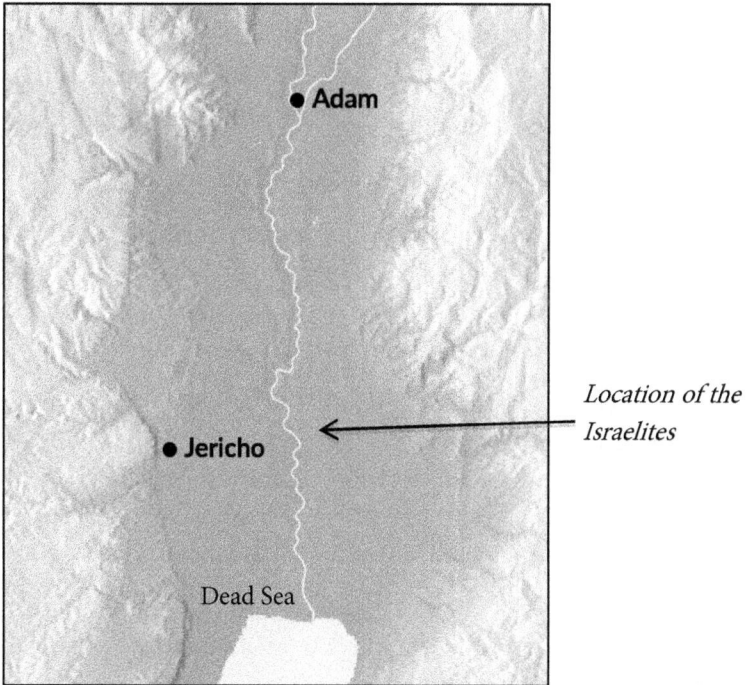

Location of the Israelites

Joshua

4. Who was to lead the people into the Land, that is, who was it that humanly speaking orchestrated the entire crossing and gave the instructions? _____

5. What does his name mean? _____

6. Who was it that the Lord exalted when this miracle and the crossing was completed? (4:14) _____

Thus, in a sense, it was the work of Joshua that caused the judgment to stop flowing from Adam!

7. What else was the Lord accomplishing when He used Joshua to perform this miracle? (3:7 and 4:14)

_____

_____

The Ark of the Covenant

8. In 3:11-13, what did God tell the people to send before them when they crossed the Jordan? _____

9. What was inside of the Ark? _____

10. What picture might the text be painting by this?

    • God's covenant people were to follow the Covenant as they entered the Land.

Summary:

If we put these textual puzzle pieces together, the following emerges:

The Lord stopped the judgment flowing down from Adam by the person and work of salvation, hinted at by the presence of the name "Joshua," which means "salvation, and forms the full Hebrew name for Yeshua. When this happened, Israel was now free to enter into their inheritance. As they entered into their inheritance, they were reminded that life for God's people would be a life lived according to Covenant.

11. How would the people be affected as a result of participating in this miraculous crossing? (3:9-11)

_____

_____

12. What effect did this crossing have on the Canaanites? (5:1)

_____

_____

13. How did God help the Israelites remember this amazing event? (Chapter 4)

_____

_____

14. It might be possible to refer to this entire event as a renewal of the covenant. If so, how might this event have functioned that way?

_____

_____

15. In general, what role do outward visible signs play in our covenant relationship with God?

_____

_____

16. Up to this point, the Lord had made three covenants with His people in human history. Each had its own outward visible reminder (a sign). These covenants are listed below. In the spaces following them, write the accompanying covenant sign and the role or purpose that it plays in helping Israel remember the covenant.

The Covenant with Noah

Sign and Purpose _____

The Covenant with Abraham

Sign and Purpose _____

The Covenant at Mount Sinai

Sign and Purpose _____

Covenant Responsibilities — Joshua Chapter 5

1. What two covenant responsibilities are brought to the forefront in Joshua chapter 5?

    a. _____

    b. _____

2. Why do you think it was essential that the Lord had Israel focus on these covenant activities just before they entered the Land?

    _____

    _____

3. Why were the Israelite men not circumcised? (5:3-7)

    _____

    _____

    _____

4. What do you think the Lord's comments to Joshua meant in 5:9 when He said, "Today I have rolled away the reproach of Egypt from you."?

    Note: Please answer this and give your own opinion and understanding before reading our suggestion below in the grey box.

    _____

    _____

    _____

> "Since the Egyptians practiced circumcision, it is not likely that 'the reproach of Egypt' refers to any inability to practice this rite in that land (cf. v. 5). It might mean that the Israelites, now re-established as the covenant people in the Land of Promise, had been delivered from their national disgrace of enslavement and homelessness."
>
> — Donald H. Madvig, *Expositor's Bible Commentary*, Comments on Joshua 5:9

5. What explanation does the text give for the origin of the place name of "Gilgal" in 5:9?

    _____

    _____

    Note: unfortunately, scholars have not yet determined the exact location of Gilgal. There are some good ideas, but precise positive identification of the archaeological site has not yet been decided upon. Maybe they will discover it tomorrow!

6. What covenant activity is the focus of 5:10-12?

    _____

    Why do you think this would be considered to be a "covenant activity?

    _____

    _____

7. Which two covenants would the activities of chapter 5 have been representative of?

    _____

Joshua 5:13-15 records an encounter Joshua had with a strange person. The following questions are about that encounter:

1. What was Joshua's location? _____

2. What might Joshua's thinking have been about at that time and in that location?

    _____

3. Who visited Joshua? How is he described? What did he have with him?

    _____

    _____

    _____

4. What did Joshua ask him? Why do you think Joshua asked him that question? (5:13)

    _____

5. What was the visitor's response in 5:14-15?

_____

_____

6. Why is that a significant response, especially for Joshua?

_____

_____

7. What did the man tell Joshua to do, and why do you think he told Joshua this?

_____

_____

8. At what event in Moshe's life did God give a similar command?

_____

_____

Is there any possible connection between these two events?

_____

_____

9. Who do you think this visitor might have been and why do you think this way? What possible evidence does the text give us to help us to identify this visitor of Joshua?

_____

_____

_____

10. What possible purpose or purposes do you think that this visitation might have served?

_____

_____

_____

_____

Before we go to the next chapter of this booklet (and the next chapters of Joshua) let us make a short notation about the dates of this story in Joshua.

1. According to 1 Kings 6:1, the year of the exodus from Egypt seems to have been 1446 BCE. Therefore, 40 years later, seems to be 1406 when the conquest began.

    Note: This is based on the scholarly assumption that the building of Solomon's Temple began in 966 BCE, at least according to many conservative Bible scholars.

2. According to 3:15, what season of this year does the story in Joshua seem to be and what is the evidence?

    _____

    _____

3. What seems to be the date of the crossing of the Jordan in 4:19?

    _____

4. What would be the date reflected in 5:10?

    _____

CHAPTER THREE

The Conquest: Claiming the Covenant Inheritance – Part 1

Joshua Chapters 6-9

Chapters 6-12 provide a summary of the actual conquest of the Promised Land. It goes without saying that many more events happened that are not recorded in the *Book of Joshua*. However, the episodes which are recorded are done so because they have special meaning to the flow of biblical history. We shall examine these things in that light. For convenience sake, we have divided this section into two chapters because there is a great amount of material. Thus, Chapter 3 of this booklet is The Conquest: Claiming the Covenant Inheritance – Part I, Joshua Chapters 6-9

The Conquest of Jericho — Joshua Chapter 6

1. Please refer to the map of Jericho in the previous chapter to answer the following question:

    Based on what you see in the map, why do you think it was necessary to begin the conquest at the city of Jericho?

    _____

    _____

2. According to 6:3-5, what was the battle plan for the capturing of Jericho?

    _____

    _____

    _____

3. What do you think of this battle plan?

    _____

    _____

4. According to this battle plan, what will be the chief weapon for Israel that will give them victory?

    _____

5. Why do you think that the text seems to stress the use of the number 7? What might we be able to learn from that use?

    _____

    _____

    _____

6. What did the Lord say to do to Jericho when it was conquered? 6:17-19

    _____

    _____

7. What were the Israelites instructed to do when they conquered the Land? (Deuteronomy 7:2)

    _____

    _____

8. What might be some possible reasons for the Lord's instructions?

    _____

    _____

> **Dr. Francis Schaeffer says:**
>
> "The city of Jericho was a sign of the first fruits. In all things the first fruits belonged to God. Jericho was the first fruits of the land; therefore, everything in it was devoted to God."
>
> — Francis Schaeffer, *Joshua*, 96,

Pictures of Jericho Archaeology

Tell Jericho, looking west.
The spies would have fled into the hills behind Jericho,
the Judean Wilderness.

A visual of how the walls of Jericho fell. We see the double wall of
Jericho. The mud bricks on top of the walls crumbled over the stone
base, allowing the Israelites to easily walk over the walls into the city.

The Conquest of Ai — Joshua 7:1-8:23

From a military point of view, the one who is on the higher elevation has greater command of the situation. Jericho was in the Jordan Valley and below sea level. By taking the city, Joshua was now in a position to control the three approaches to the higher elevation, the Central Mountain. Thus, the next step was to take the outpost of Ai, another fortress city at the top of one of the ascents to the Central Mountains. Although the location of Ai is pictured in the black circle in the map below, in reality, scholars still are not sure about its exact location, though there are few good suggestions. Whatever has been suggested, it is close to the Ai on this map.

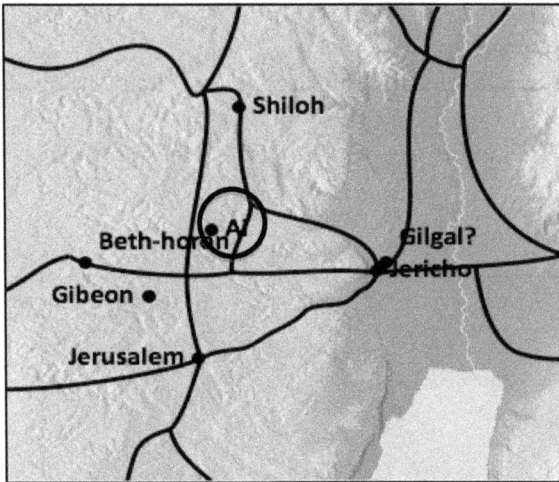

1. What happened in the aftermath of the Jericho victory? (7:1)

    _____

    _____

2. Describe what happened to the Israelites at Ai, according to 7:2-5.

    _____

    _____

3. Why did this happen? (7:1; 10-13)

    _____

    _____

4. What was Joshua's response to what happened? (7:6-9)

_____

_____

5. What might this teach us about prayer?

_____

_____

_____

6. In 7:20, against whom did Achan say he sinned?

_____

7. In 7:21, what was it that Achan stole?

_____

8. What did Achan say was his motive in stealing?

_____

_____

9. Where did he say he found these things?

_____

Considering where he found these items, what do you think might have been going through his mind when he saw them?

_____

_____

_____

10. How did the Lord solve the problem? 7:14-26

_____

_____

_____

11. Why do you think the text mentions the culprit's name specifically, instead of being very general?

_____

_____

_____

12. What might this say about the nature of a covenant community and the responsibility we have to one another? (7:25)

_____

_____

13. Where was Achan buried? Why is it called that name? (7:26)

_____

_____

14. What was the strategy that Joshua had to win the second battle against Ai? (8:1-9)

_____

_____

_____

15. Why did God grant victory this time? What can we learn from this about living in covenant community together?

_____

_____

_____

16. What was the strategic victory that Israel gained by taking Ai, as well as Jericho?

_____

_____

_____

The Renewing of the Covenant — Joshua 8:30-35

> **Memory Verse:**
>
> **Joshua 8:35** – "There was not a word from all that Moses had commanded which Joshua did not read before all the assembly of Israel with the women and the little ones and the strangers who were walking among them."

1. What did Joshua do after the victory at Ai in 8:30-35?

    _____

2. On what authority did Joshua do this? See Deuteronomy 27:12-14.

    _____

    _____

3. Where was this done? 8:30, 33

    Find this location on a Bible map. What seems to be the strategic advantage for doing this event at this location?

    _____

    _____

    What might be another reason why this event was done at this location? (See Genesis 12:5-7)

    _____

    _____

4. What was a central component to this ceremony? (8:32-35)

    _____

5. What implications might 8:35 have for the traditional Jewish concept called Oral Torah?

    _____

    _____

    _____

6.   Why do you think Joshua led Israel in a covenant renewal at this particular time in the conquest of the Land?

_____

_____

_____

The Covenant with the Gibeonites — Joshua Chapter 9

1.   How were the inhabitants of the Land beginning to respond to Israel's conquests? (9:1-2)

_____

_____

Note: In 9:2, many English translations read that they acted "with one accord" (NASB, KJV, JPS). The Hebrew says they acted "with one mouth."

2.   What did the people of Gibeon do? _____

_____

Why did they do this? (9:24-25)

_____

_____

3.   In the space below, give your opinion about whether Israel was right or wrong for making a covenant with the Gibeonites. Consider the following passages: Deuteronomy 7:2; Deuteronomy 20:10-15; and Deuteronomy 20:16-18; and Joshua 9:18-19

4. Francis Schaeffer wrote, when discussing this incident in Joshua, "an oath made in the name of the God of holiness is to be kept with holy hands." (*Joshua*, 148, see bibliography) Was he right or wrong? Were the Israelites right or wrong in keeping the promise they made to the Gibeonites? Explain.

5. Please note the location of Gibeon on the map. Notice the distance that it is to Gilgal (over 15 miles, about 25 km). Thus, the Gibeonites were not that far from where Israel was encamped, but they deceived Israel into thinking that they came from quite a distance.

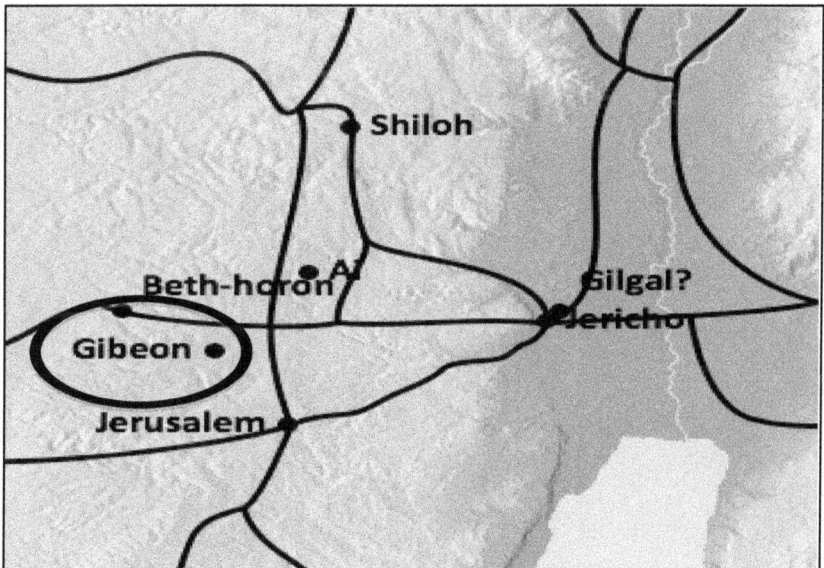

CHAPTER FOUR

The Conquest: Claiming the Covenant Inheritance – Part 2

Joshua Chapters 10-12

The Southern Campaign — Joshua Chapter 10

> **Memory Verse:**
>
> **Joshua 10:14** – "There was no day like that before it or after it, when the Lord listened to the voice of a man; for the Lord fought for Israel."

1. What new development brought the Israelites back into battle? (10:1-5)

    _____

    _____

2. What cities/kings were involved in this military activity?

    _____

3. According to 10:9, how did Joshua and the Israelite army arrive to Gibeon?

    _____

    _____

    _____

    Can you guess approximately how old Joshua was at this time? _____

4. The following are pictures of how the terrain looked where Joshua had to march to get to Gibeon, climbing over 3,000 ft (915 m), at night, over rugged terrain for about 15 miles (24 km), walking along steep drops with no rest and no light. What does all of this speak about the strength and fitness of both Joshua and the Israelite army?

    _____

    _____

5. After the battle at Gibeon, where did Joshua chase the Amorites? (10:10-13)

    _____

6. In what ways did the Lord enable the Israelites to have victory over the Amorites? (See 10:10-14)

_____

_____

_____

7. Find the following on the map below:
   - The location of the 5 Canaanite/Amorite cities
   - The location of Gibeon, of Ai, and of Jericho
   - The "escape route" of the Canaanites \ Gibeon?

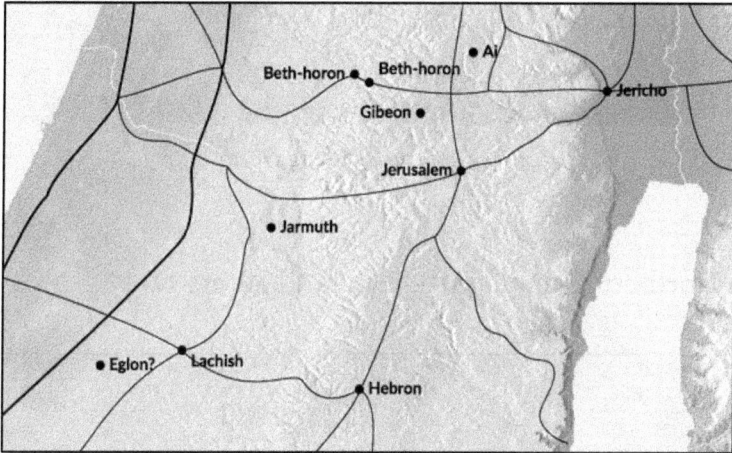

8. Based on what you see on the map, and what the text says in 10:40-43, what seems to be a major strategic value of Joshua winning the battle of Gibeon? What geographic area was now in the hands of Israel when the whole affair was finished? _____

_____

_____

9. When we consider what happened at the battle of Gibeon, and its aftermath in chapter 10, in what way might we apply Romans 8:28 to the entire story of the Israelites and the Gibeonites in chapters 9-10? Explain why it might be good to see the story in this way.

_____

_____

Gibeon, Looking North

The Northern Campaign — Joshua Chapters 11-12

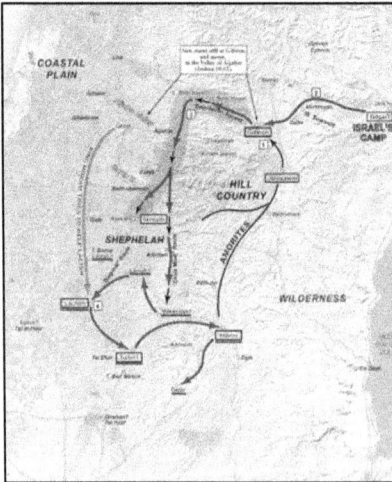

Israel's Southern Campaign   *Israel's Northern Campaign*

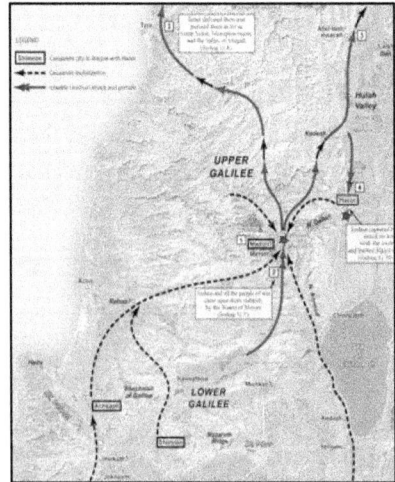

Maps: Courtesy of William Schlegel, Satellite Bible Atlas

1. Look at the following passage and see if you can discern a pattern, or patterns, emerging that tells us how the Lord developed the strategy of taking the Land: 2:9-11; 5:1; 9:1-2; 10:1-5; 11:1-5; 11:20

   _____

   _____

   _____

2. Compare the 4 recorded battles thus far: Jericho, Ai, Gibeon and the Amorites, and Merom (chapter 11). How are they similar, and how do they differ?

   _____

   _____

   _____

3. As time went on, the challenges to Joshua increased in difficulty. In what ways do we see that in the Northern Campaign?

   _____

   _____

   In what ways can this principle help us in the struggles we face in our daily lives? _____

   _____

   _____

4. According to 11:6-8, what was the divine strategy that would be used to defeat this huge Canaanite army?

   _____

   _____

   Note: Jabin — King of Hazor. Jabin was possibly the name of his family dynasty or perhaps a generic name for the ruler of Hazor.

5. The Canaanites used chariots (advanced weapons) to fight the Israelites. What does God's Word say about the importance of using advanced military technology? (Deuteronomy 17:16; 2 Samuel 8:4; and Isaiah 31:1)

_____

_____

_____

THE CHIEF PARTICIPANTS IN THE NORTHERN CAMPAIGN

Canaanites — lived in the lowlands such as seacoast, the Jordan Valley, and the great valleys of the Galilee

Amorites — often used as a generic name for western Semites who lived in the hill country of Canaan

Jebusites —The ethnic name of a people dwelling in the hills (Numbers 13:29; Joshua 11:3) round about Jerusalem (Joshua 15:8; 18:16). Descended from the third son of Canaan.

Hivites — One of the sons of Canaan (Genesis 10:17, their principal location was in the Lebanon hills (Judges 3:3) and the Hermon range as far as the valley leading to Hamat.

Perizzites — They were apparently hill-dwellers in Canaan. Some suggest that the term "Perizzites" to be as "villagers." The fact that Genesis 10:15ff. does not name Perizzites among Canaan's "sons" supports this possibility.

Hittites — In the Tanakh, the Hittites are a great nation which gave its name to the whole region of Syria "from the wilderness and this Lebanon as far as the great river, the river Euphrates, all the land of the Hittites to the Great Sea toward the going down of the sun" (Joshua 1:4).

Hazor — It was the most important Canaanite city in the north and was a fortified city about 10 miles north of the lake of Galilee. Hazor, Jericho, and Ai were the only cities burnt in Joshua's conquest.

Some two centuries later Hazor was fortified, together with Jerusalem, Megiddo and Gezer, by Solomon when he was organizing his kingdom (1 Kings 9:15). In the 8th century, in the time of Pekah of Israel, Tiglath-pileser III of Assyria came and destroyed the city and carried off its remaining inhabitants to Assyria (2 Kings 15:29).

Hazor

It is almost in passing that we read in Joshua 11:10, "Then Joshua turned back at that time, and captured Hazor and struck its king with the sword; for Hazor formerly was the head of all these kingdoms." There was a good amount of material about the capture of Jericho, Ai, Gibeon, and even about the Battle of Merom. Yet, in one short sentence we read that Joshua took Hazor. It almost seems like taking Hazor was incidental, the victory of a sleepy off-the-beaten-track town.

However, Joshua 11:10 provides us an important piece of information about the importance of Hazor. We read in 11:10 that Hazor was, "formerly head of all these kingdoms." Archaeology has helped us to understand this description. Look at the following pictures before reading on.

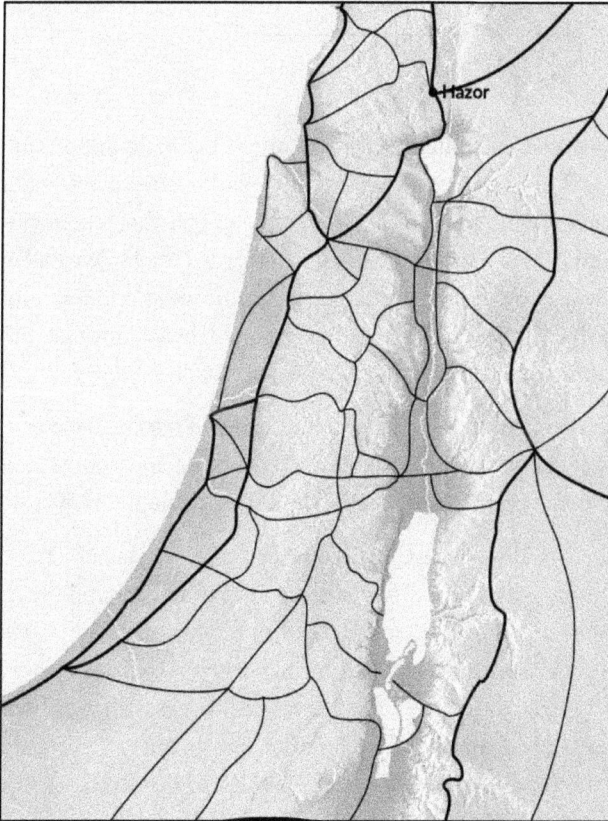

Map indicating the location of Hazor, in the Galilee.

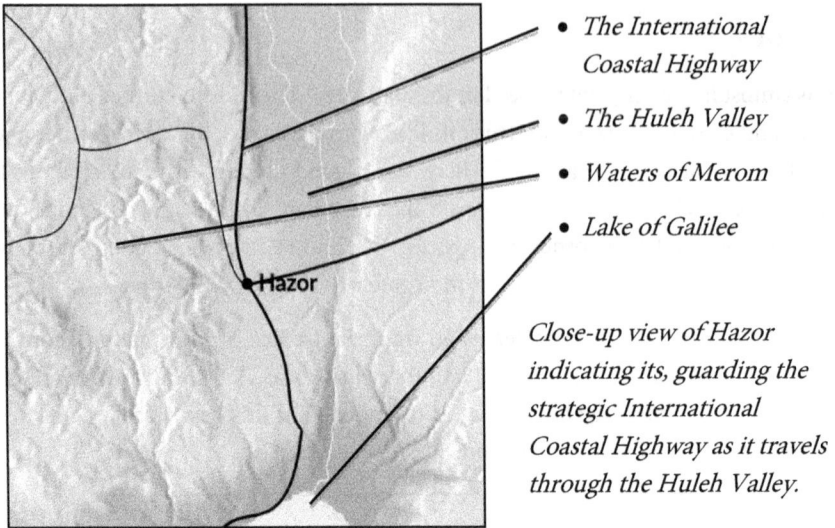

- *The International Coastal Highway*
- *The Huleh Valley*
- *Waters of Merom*
- *Lake of Galilee*

Close-up view of Hazor indicating its, guarding the strategic International Coastal Highway as it travels through the Huleh Valley.

It is now known that, in reality, Hazor was one of the most important cities in that part of the world. It was situated right on the world-renown International Coastal Highway, which connected Africa, Asia, and Europe, thus enhancing Israel as a geographic land bridge. Furthermore, Hazor guarded the Huleh Valley, a source of water, surrounded by fertile agriculture. All invading armies, especially from Mesopotamia (like Assyria and Babylon) entered Israel through this valley and along this road, enhancing the strategic value of Hazor.

Archaeology has enhanced our perception of Hazor. Both the Bible and archaeology confirm that Joshua burnt only three cities: Jericho, Ai, and Hazor. He did so under the command of the Lord and because of the strategic value of each city.

Today, Hazor is the largest archeological site in Israel, the largest *tell.* Unfortunately, the very science that has helped us to understand the importance of Hazor, is also the source of much conflict concerning the city. Respectable archaeologists offer conflicting views on when Joshua destroyed Hazor. Some (like Yigael Yadin, James Hoffmeier, and Amnon Ben-Tor) say that the evidence points to what is referred to as "Late Date" (sometime in the 13th century BCE) while others (Bryant Wood, Charles Aling, and Douglas Petrovich) assert the evidence points to an early date (14th century BCE).

The dating of the Israelite destruction of Hazor also affects one's understanding of the date of the Exodus. A late date conflicts with the biblical dating (1446 BCE) while the early date is fully compatible with the biblical information. Thus, the side one takes on the dating of the Israelite destruction of Hazor influences one's perception of biblical data.

We cannot deal with the issue here. Since we are committed to defending the absolute integrity of the Bible, we favor the early date for Hazor's destruction. Fortunately, much work has been done to challenge liberal minded scholars who seek to undermine the integrity of the Scriptures. One might want to explore the website of the Associates for Biblical Research (see Bibliography), for example, to read papers dealing with solid evidence. We offer this extended quote from an excellent essay dealing with this subject by Dr. Douglas Petrovich (see Bibliography). He writes:

"This conclusion, borne out by the evidence presented in the preceding discussion, strongly supports the chronological framework of the early-exodus position, and thus the literal interpretation of numbers such as 480 in 1 Kings 6:1. Biblical scholars and teachers would do well to give the biblical text its full day in court before acquiescing to the interpretations of archaeologists or other scholars who use arguments from silence to make claims such as the Israelites' inability to have occupied the Promised Land before the 13th century BC, especially since such conclusions fan the flames of non-inerrantist, liberal scholars determined to undermine the historicity of the Bible. As [Israeli Archaeologist] Aharoni warned, 'Don't reject the historicity of the Biblical text so easily'. The Bible should be interpreted literally, whenever possible, even though popular scholarship may tempt biblical scholars to take the easy road by reverting to allegorism when interpretive difficulties are encountered."

Aerial view of Tell Hazor, looking northeast

Down with the Anakim! — Joshua Chapters 11:21-23

1. Who were the Anakim?

    a. Possible translations of the word "Anak"

        - "The long-necked people"

        - "The neck-chain people" (from the rings worn by them or their animals)

        - "Giants: Septuagint (LXX) γιγάντες in Deuteronomy 1:28

        - Related to Greek ἄναξ — a Philistine word "designating an official position"

    b. A section of the pre-Israelite population of Canaan, especially around Hebron

2. What role did the Anakim have in Israel's initial rejection of the Land in Numbers 13:22, 28, 32-33; Deuteronomy 1:28?

    _____

    _____

3. In light of the above, why do you think that Joshua makes special mention of the Anakim in 11:21-23?

    _____

    _____

4. Where did the Anakim eventually settle after Joshua defeated them?

    _____

    What people group eventually settled in those locations?

    _____

    — This indicates that the Anakim were perhaps associated with those people.

Summary of the Conquest 11:23-chapter 12

1. How much of the Land did Joshua conquer, according to 11:23? _____

    _____

What might this tell us about the use of and meaning of the Hebrew word translated all, *kal,* כֹל?

_____

_____

2. What did Israel do after they were finished with that phase of conquest? (11:23) **Note:** The Hebrew word translated "rest" is the word "quiet", *shaqat,* שקט. What does it mean to have quiet after major activity like the Israelites experienced? Why is it necessary? How can we have such "quiet"?

_____

3. What are the different geographical regions of Israel listed that Israel conquered in 12:7-8? Try finding these regions on the map below. You will probably have to use a good Bible atlas to do this, but that is part of proper Bible study!

a. _____

b. _____

c. _____

d. _____

e. _____

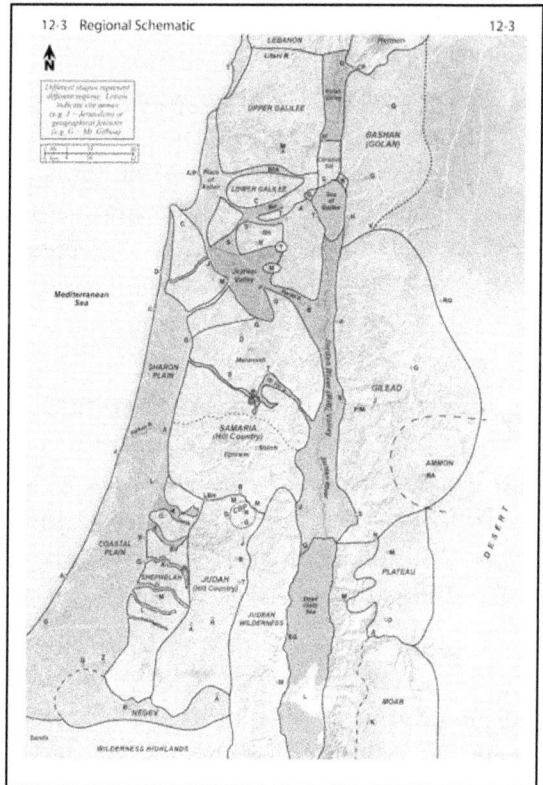

12-3 Regional Schematic   12-3

As we conclude this section about the conquest, what are some things that we have learned about God?

_____

_____

_____

Geographic Notes from Chapter 12

The *Book of Joshua* provides many geographic place names for us to consider. As we go through the book, we realize that some of these names are simply unknown to us. Yet, other names are known, though by different names. Here are some of them that we see in chapter 12 of Joshua:

12:35 — The Aravah (*ha'aravah*, הערבה)
We usually think of the Aravah as that wasteland south of the Dead Sea, which is how the word is used today. However Joshua is indicating that the Aravah was also south of the Sea of Galilee.

Sea of Kinnerot (*yam kinrot*, ים כנרות)
Here we find an ancient name for the Sea of Galilee: Yam Kinnerot. This would correspond to the modern Israeli name for the lake, Lake Kinneret. For interest sake, notice that this body of fresh water is referred to in Hebrew as a *yam* (ים). A yam can be any body of water, except for a river, such as an ocean, sea, or in this case a lake. Hence, the so-called "Sea of Galilee" is not a salt-water ocean, but a mid-sized fresh water inland lake somewhere between 686 ft. (209 m) and 705 ft. (215 m) below sea level.

Sea of the Arabah (*yam ha'aravah*, ים הערבה)
The context tells us that this Aravah is close to the so-called "Dead Sea." As stated above, in today's Israel the land south of the Dead Sea is referred to as the Aravah. However, this use of Aravah hints at the possibility that the land just north of the Dead Sea can also biblically be called Aravah, as well as the land just south of Lake Kinneret. Hence, biblically Aravah is much larger than today's use of the term.

Salt Sea (*yam hamelach*, ים המלח)
"Salt Sea" is an ancient name for what we call the "Dead Sea" today. Notice that it also is referred to as a yam. Indeed, it is also an inland lake, not an ocean. The name "Salt Sea" (Yam haMelach) is how modern Israel calls this body of water, located over 1,400 feet (430 m) below sea level.

12:5 — The Bashan (*habashan*, הבשן)

Bashan is a very fertile plateau east of Lake Kinneret, extending east for about 25 miles (about 40 km) to modern-day Syria, north of the Yarmuk River and south of Mount Hermon. Today it is called the Golan Heights. It used to be volcanic, which accounts for the fertile soil.

12:7 — Valley of Lebanon (*habik'at halevanon*, בקעת הלבנון)

Today, this would be in modern Lebanon. Back then, there was no political entity called "Lebanon." Yet, there are several biblical passages that would suggest the area of most of modern Lebanon was to be part of the God-given promised land to Israel. Moreover, the "valley" of Lebanon is called in Hebrew bik'ah (בקעה). Today, the Rift Valley, a major geographic feature that extends from Africa in the south, through Israel (where it is called the "Jordan Valley" extends into modern Lebanon and is called the Bik'ah Valley. The word "bik'ah" itself means "valley" and differs from other Hebrew words translated valley in that it is a kind of a large and wide U-shaped valley with gentle sides.

Seir (שעיר) — This is a name that refers to one of the slopes of Mount Hermon.

CHAPTER FIVE

Finally:

The Covenant Inheritance!

Joshua Chapters 13-21

> **Memory Verse:**
>
> **Joshua 13:1** – "Now Joshua was old and advanced in years when the Lord said to him, 'You are old and advanced in years, and very much of the land remains to be possessed'."

We have been focusing on the idea of covenant as we travel through the *Book of Joshua*. The Torah informed us that God made two covenants with Israel, one with Abraham and then another with Abraham's descents at Mount Sinai. Both covenants work together to form this complete picture: God gave promises out of His grace to Israel via our father Abraham, yet for Israel to experience fruitfulness and enjoyment of those promises, they were instructed to live by the instructions of the covenant-making God that He taught at Mount Sinai.

The *Book of Joshua* is a tale of how both covenants come together. Israel had a covenantal right to the Land and a covenantal responsibility to be faithful to the Mount Sinai covenant when they lived in the Land. In this present chapter in our study booklet, we will examine Joshua chapters 13-21 and explore some of the ramifications of what it was for Israel as a whole to actually begin to live in their inheritance.

Please refer to the following map to see a visual on approximately where the tribal borders lie.

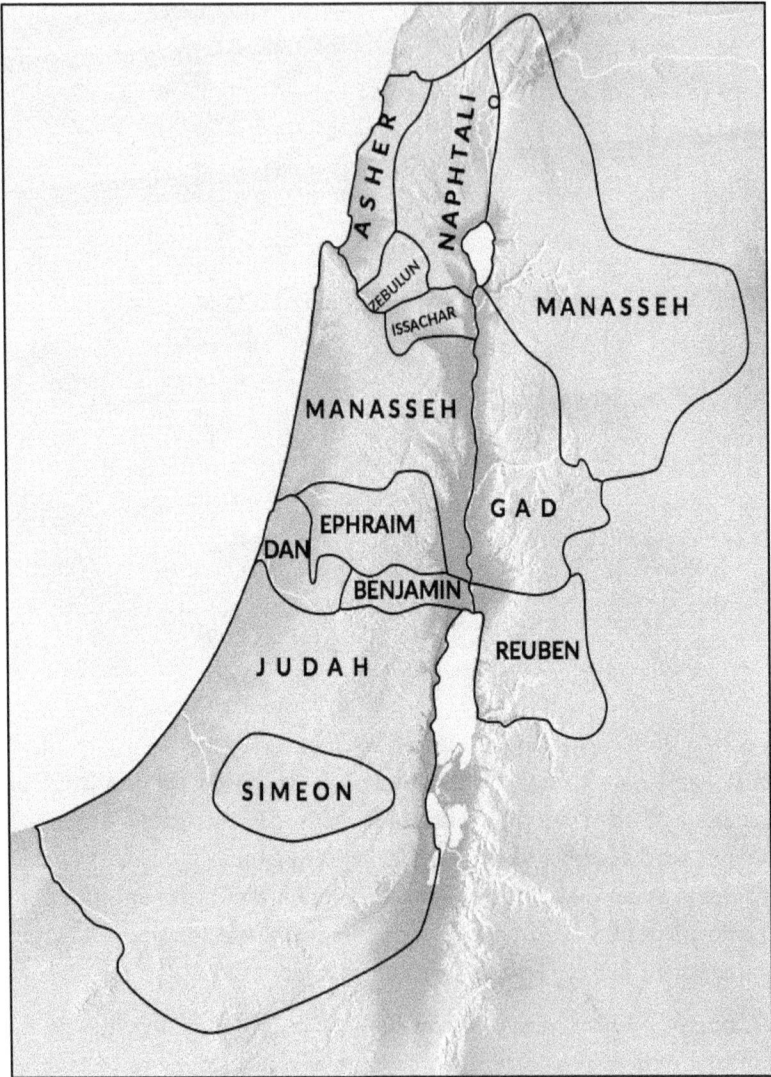

The Land That Remains: Joshua 13:1-13

1. In 13:1 we see a comment about Joshua's age at the time when he finished his part of the conquest. A typical English translation of 13:1 says, "Joshua was old and advanced in years" (NASB). The Hebrew uses an idiom that literally says, "old and coming into the days." No matter how one phrases it, Joshua was

getting to be an old man, which means that for much of the conquest he was quite advanced in years. We have read in 12 chapters how Joshua spent his "golden years!" How do you plan to spend your advanced years? What lessons can we glean from the "old man" about how to spend the latter part of one's life for the Lord?

_____

_____

_____

_____

2. In chapter 13 we see a record of the land still to conquer. Why do you think the text of Joshua provides us with this information?

_____

_____

_____

Why do you think that God did not use Joshua to lead Israel in conquering this land?

_____

_____

_____

Note: In Joshua 13:3 we read "…five lords of the Philistines: the Gazite, the Ashdodite, the Ashkelonite, the Gittite, the Ekronite…" First, note that this is the first mention in the Bible of the famous 5 Philistine cities: Gaza, Ashkelon, Ashdod, Gath, and Ekron. Second, bear in mind that historically the Philistines did not come to Canaan *en masse* until about 1200 BCE, which would be about 150 years after these events took place in the *Book of Joshua*. What we see, therefore, is what might be a good example of simple scribal updating of factual information. This does not take away from the divine inspiration of the Scriptures, nor does it deny that Joshua might have been the author of this book. Rather, it simply indicates that from time to time scribes updated important factual information.

3. It is easy to get lost in the text with all of the place names that, for the average reader outside of Israel, might seem rather meaningless. Let us, therefore step

back from the text a little and observe the big picture. When we do so, we can ask a simple question about the text of Joshua: What might some of the purposes be in providing the geographic details that chapters 13-21 mention? Let us suggest some.

a.   These chapters provide physical proof that what God promised the Patriarchs has come true — God meant what He said.

- How do they provide such proof?

_____

_____

_____

b.   The information recorded in these chapters might provide what could be viewed "title deeds" for each tribe.

- If that is true, then how so? What function does a title deed perform? In what way can the information be construed to be tribal title deeds?

_____

_____

_____

c.   Each tribe and individual in that tribe would have heard he boundaries and thought, "Yes! This is my land and the land for my family!"

- How do you think each tribal member would have felt? What do you think they would have thought about their God?

_____

_____

_____

Moshe, Joshua and The Tribal Inheritances

We would like to suggest one more possible purpose for this detailed information in these land allotment chapters. Perhaps they might provide a means to verify Moshe's prophecies about each tribe. If so, this would be yet a further connection between Moshe and Joshua, Deuteronomy and the *Book of Joshua*.

Some of Moshe's final words to Israel are recorded in the concluding chapters of Deuteronomy. Just as he was beginning to make his fateful trek up the mountains of Moav that overlook the plain where the Israelites were encamped before crossing the Jordan, Moshe passed by each tribe and spoke a final blessing to them. While Deuteronomy 33:1 calls these words "blessings," in reality, they are blessings that also double as prophecies for each tribe.

In Joshua 13, Joshua begins to record the land inheritance for each tribe by beginning with the Transjordan tribes first: Reuven, Gad, and half of the tribe of Manasseh. Then, starting in chapter 14 and continuing for a few chapters, the land inheritance for each of the other tribes is listed.

We would like to compare the blessings/prophecies that Moshe spoke for each tribe with their tribal location to see if there might be a connection. After all, the blessings in Deuteronomy basically follow a geographical order, working from the east to south then toward the north. Thus, geography seems to play an important role in understanding the tribal locations and Moshe's blessings. One more point before we begin.

Please understand that we are not attempting to give an exegetical and expositional exegesis of Deuteronomy 33. We will leave many of Moshe's words to the tribes out of our discussion. We are only concerned with how we can understand some of what Moshe said in light of the tribal inheritances as Joshua records them. Let us see how this works. We shall study the land allotment to the tribes in the order that they appear in Joshua.

Reuven: Joshua 13:15-23

1. Where is Reuven's tribal location? (Joshua 13:15-23)

---

2. Because of his tribal location, with hostile Edom on the south and the harsh desert on the east with its warlike nomads, what would Reuven have been in need of?

---

3. Hence, according to Deuteronomy 33:6, what is Moshe promising for Reuven?

Gad: Joshua 13:24-28

1. Where is Gad's tribal location? (Joshua 13:15-23)

   _____

2. Because of his tribal location, with the desert on his east and living, therefore on a border, like Reuven does, how would Gad apparently handle this position according to Moshe's prediction about him in Deuteronomy 33:20-21?

   _____

   _____

   _____

   _____

3. A Note about Gad:

   — The fact that Gad chose the territory east of the Jordan for his inheritance, prompted Rashi to furnish an interesting interpretation of the first part of Moshe's blessing, "he dwells like a lion, tearing off arm and even head." Rashi suggests that this reflects the military strength of Gad because he, i.e., his land, was adjacent to the border. That is why he is compared to lions, for all who are adjacent to the border must be mighty.

Manasseh and Ephraim: 13:29-32 and Chapters 16-17

Half of the tribe of Manasseh would dwell on the east side of the Jordan. The other half would inherit land on the west side. Moshe included both sons of Joseph in the same blessing, Manasseh and Ephraim. In like manner, Joshua delineates their tribal inheritance by referring to them as the sons of Joseph (16:1), although he goes on to differentiate between Manasseh and Ephraim.

1. Where is the tribal location of both Manasseh and Ephraim? (Joshua 13:29-32 and Chapters 16-17)

   _____

2. What is the nature of Moshe's blessing for the sons of Joseph? (Deuteronomy 33:13-17)

   _____

   _____

Note: Only those who know the geography of Israel would be able to understand the nature of Moshe's prediction in relation to their tribal location.

— The main thrust of Moshe's blessing concerns itself with the land of Joseph, the tribal land area given to his two sons, Ephraim and Manasseh. They were being blessed with the best gifts of the land and its fullness. That is most certainly true! With protective mountains separated sometimes by wide and fertile valleys, the central part of Israel is one of the most beautiful and sought-after places in Israel to live.

Judah: Joshua Chapter 15

1. According to Joshua 15, we learn more details about Judah's inheritance than any other tribe. Why do you think that might be so?

    _____

    _____

    _____

2. Given what we know about the tribal location, with borders on three of its sides and its position of leadership among the Israelites, to what do you think Moshe was referring when he said in Deuteronomy 33:7, "And may You be a help against his adversaries?"

    _____

    _____

    Who is the "You" in 33:7? _____

Benjamin: Joshua 18:11-28

1. Who was on Benjamin's south and who was on his north? (Joshua 18:11)

    _____

2. According to Moshe's blessing in Deuteronomy 33:17, where would Benjamin dwell?

    _____

    What did Moshe say he would be in need of?

    _____

3. To whose "shoulders" is Moshe referring and why would Moshe word the blessing like this?

_____

_____

_____

Simeon: 19:1-9

1. According to Joshua 19:1, where was Simeon's inheritance?

_____

_____

2. What was the reason for this, according to Joshua 19:9?

_____

_____

3. Moshe's blessing —

Curiously, Moshe does not speak a separate blessing for the tribe of Simeon. Naturally, this oddity has sparked a variety of explanations that commentators have offered. It would, indeed, have been logical for Simeon and Judah to share a blessing since Simeon's territory was within Judah's. Moreover, it is possible that Simeon was intentionally omitted precisely because its territory was within Judah's and it was an insignificant tribe.

Both Simeon and Levi were the patriarchs who had led the slaughter against the Shechemites in Genesis 34. It seems that in Jacob's prophecy regarding his sons' future, recorded in Genesis 49, they are judged by being kept from possession of territory in the conquered land.

The fact remains, however, that Joshua 19 does record a tribal inheritance for Simeon. He is not excluded from his brothers!

Zebulun 19:10-16 and Issachar Joshua 19:17-23

1. According to Joshua 19:10-16, Zebulun's and Issachar's tribal locations were right in the heart of the Galilee. In fact, the tribal location for the town of Nazareth was Zebulun, where Yeshua grew up and Isachar's tribe bordered on the Lake of Galilee.

2. According to Joshua their inheritance came right after each other and they bordered on each other very closely. What might the record of their birth in Genesis 35:23 have to do with this closeness? _____

_____

3. Moshe did not have much to say regarding Zebulun and Issachar in 33:18. However, what *did* he did say about them? How would that have been appropriate for their tribal locations?

_____

_____

_____

_____

Asher: 19:24-31

1. According to Joshua 19:27, which tribe bordered Asher?

_____

2. According to Joshua 19:29, what was part of the western border of Asher?

_____

3. Moshe says that Asher will be blessed. Accordingly, Deuteronomy 33:34 says that Asher will "_____." In addition, he will be blessed with iron and bronze. It seems that all of this speaks of a very lucrative trade business where Asher exported its olive oil from its port on the coast and imported iron and bronze. We say this because of Asher's location in the Galilee, where abundant olives were grown and exported through one of Israel's few ports located in Asher.

Naphtali: 19:32-39

1. Joshua 19:34 says that part of Naphtali's border was with which tribes?

_____

2. In Joshua 19:35, which famous city was within Naphtali's borders? Compare this name with Joshua 12:3.

_____

3. This means that Naphtali shared a border with what important geographic feature/location in the Galilee?

    _____

4. What did Moshe predict for Naphtali in Deuteronomy 33:23?

    _____

5. Given Naphtali's location and what was within his tribal territory, in what ways do you think the Lord would bring blessing to Naphtali? How would Isaiah 9:1 (English translation, 8:23 in the Hebrew text) add to this understanding?

    _____

    _____

    _____

Dan: 19:40-48

1. According to Joshua 19:41-46, where was the location of the tribe of Dan originally supposed to be? You can look up the cities in a Bible atlas.

    _____

2. What happened to the tribe of Dan in Joshua 19:47?

    _____

    In what part of the Land was this new location?

    _____

3. This new location might help us to understand something rather enigmatic that Moshe predicts in Deuteronomy 33:22. According to this verse, where would Dan's final home be; near which part of Israel?

    _____

4. One needs a little Hebrew to understand the rest of what Moshe said. Here is how it goes:

    - "Lion's whelp" — *gur aryeh* (גור אריה). This is a young lion.

    - Leshem (Joshua 19:47) is also referred to as Laish in Judges 18:7

    - Laish (ליש) — is an unusual word which also means a young lion.

However, Laish was also the name of the Canaanite city which the Danites conquered and claimed for their own — in close proximity to Bashan.

5. Hence, Joshua's and Judges account of the tribal location of Dan explains Moshes' very strange prediction for the Danites.

Levi: 18:7 and other places

1. According to Joshua 18:7, where would the tribal area be for the tribe of Levi?

_____

What is the reason given for this?

_____

2. In contrast, Moshe provides a rather long blessing for the tribe of Levi in Deuteronomy 33:8-11. According to Moshe's words, what would be the different tasks assigned to the Levites?

a. 33:8 — _____

b. 33:10 — _____

c. 33:10 — _____

d. 33:10 — _____

Other Inheritances

Another Hill For an Old Man — Joshua 14:6-15

1. Which tribal allotment is listed in chapter 14?

_____

2. Who is included with this tribe? (14:6-15)

_____

3. From which people was Caleb? (14:6)

_____

4.   What was the origin of these people according to Genesis 15:18-19

_____

5.   That means that Caleb was not a physical descendant of Jacob. What does this tell us about the Israelites? What can this teach us about who the Lord includes in His covenants? _____

_____

_____

6.   According to 14:10, how old was Caleb?

7.   What is Caleb asking for in 14:11-12? _____

On what basis does he make his request? (14:6-10)

_____

8.   We ask the same question that we asked when we studied Joshua's age: How do we plan to spend our older years?

_____

_____

9.   How does Caleb describe himself physically in 14:11?

_____

_____

10.   What can we do to ensure as much as possible that we will be just as able to do the Lord's work when we are Caleb's age?

_____

_____

Memory Verse:

Joshua 14:10 – "Now behold, the Lord has caused me to live, just as He spoke, these forty-five years, from the time that the Lord spoke this word to Moses, when Israel walked in the wilderness; and now behold today, I am eighty-five years old."

Don't Forget the Women!   Joshua 17:3-6

1. Who was it that asked Joshua and the priest Eleazar for an inheritance in Joshua 17:3-6?

   _____

2. Normally an inheritance was left for sons. Why did they ask for an inheritance?

   _____

3. What can this teach us about how God cares for women?

   _____

   _____

4. On what basis did they make their claim and on what basis did they receive their claim? (17:4)

   _____

5. What do the following passages all have in common?

   Joshua 11:15, 23; 12:1-6; 14:5; 14:6; 17:4

   _____

   _____

   What can this tell us about the continuity of the Torah?

   _____

   _____

Francis Schaeffer said:
"The fact that Joshua's generation accepted the Pentateuch as authoritative is more than a mere breath of fresh air in the heavy smog which surrounds present liberal scholarly discussion. To the Israelites, the canon [of Scripture] was not just academic, not merely theological, but practical. Joshua and the people had a continuity of authority as they moved through history. The book was to be their environment, their mentality."

— Francis Schaeffer, *Joshua*, 32,

A Change of Scenery - Joshua 18:1

1. Where does the text say that the Israelites gathered together in 18:1?

    _____

2. Up to this point, where had their main camp been?

    _____

3. Why do you think they made this change?

    _____

4. The map below shows the location of Shiloh, Gibeon, and the approximate location of Gilgal. The black lines represent major routes.

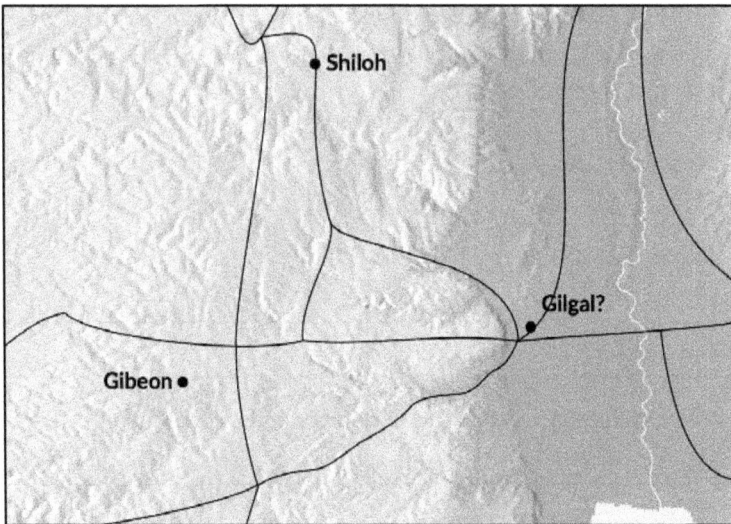

Special Cities: Joshua Chapters 20-21

Cities of Refuge - Joshua Chapter 20

1. According to Joshua 20:1-2, what else did Moshe instruct Joshua to do in the Land?

    _____

    _____

2.   What was the purpose for these cities? (20:3)

_____

3.   According to 20:4-6, how were these cities to function?

_____

4.   Why do you suppose the Lord instructed Israel to designate such places? What does this teach us about the nature of God and His justice and mercy?

_____

_____

5.   The map below shows the location of these cities of refuge.

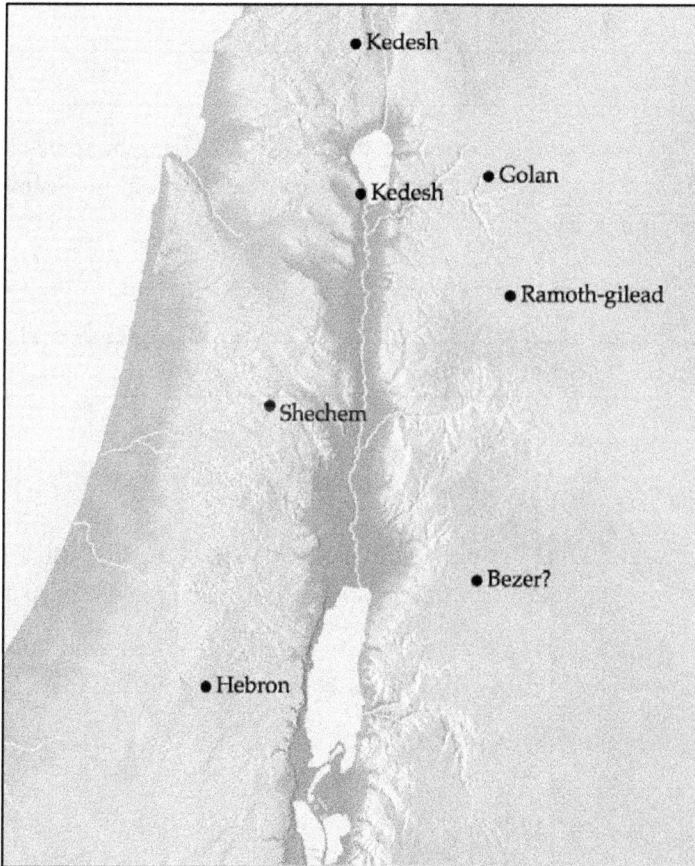

Cities for the Levites:　Joshua Chapter 21

1.　In Joshua 21:1-3, what were the Levites asking for and on what basis were they making this request?

_____

_____

2.　What were they planning on doing with this land? (21:2)

_____

_____

3.　How do we reconcile what we find here in Joshua 21 and the Levitical cities with the pronouncement of discipline found in Genesis 49:7?

_____

_____

4.　Was the designation of cities for the Levites a blessing or something that should not have been done, according to the prophecy in Genesis 49:7? Explain your answer.

_____

_____

_____

Memory Verses:

Joshua 21:43 – "So the Lord gave to Israel all the land which He swore to give to their fathers, and they possessed it and lived in it.

Joshua 21:45 – "And a word from every good word did not fall which the Lord had made to the house of Israel; all came to pass."

CHAPTER SIX

The Finale:

Joshua Chapters 22-24

Memory Verses:

Joshua 23:6, 8 – "Be very strong, then, to guard and do all that is written in the book of the Torah of Moshe, so that you may not turn aside from it to the right hand or to the left...for if only you will cling to the Lord your God, just as you have done to this day."

More to Do!

1. In Joshua 18:3, Joshua exhorts Israel to take the rest of the Land, in doing so, what did he ask Israel?

   _____

   _____

2. What is one reason why Israel could not drive all of the Canaanites out of the Land? (Joshua 15:63 and 17:12)

   _____

   _____

3. Instead of driving all of them out, what did Israel do to them? (Joshua 17:13)

   _____

   _____

4. What, then, was the second reason why the Israelites did not drive out the Canaanites? (Joshua 17:13)

_____

5. Thus, we see an example of why many of God's people come short of doing what the Lord asks of them. There are two reasons that we can glean from above:

    a. _____

    b. _____

6. As time went on, after Joshua was gone, the same problem persisted among the Israelites. However, more difficulties arose which made it even more difficult for them to take hold of their covenantal possession. Read Judges 2:21-3:2. Why did the Lord say that not all Canaanites would be handed over to Joshua and Israel at once?

_____

_____

Going Home!   Joshua Chapter 22:1-9

1. In Joshua 22:1-6, 8, what did Joshua tell the tribes of Transjordan to do, and why did he say they could do it?

_____

_____

2. Describe their behavior when they fought with their brothers. (22:3)

_____

_____

3. On what biblical basis could they go to their homes? (22:4,9)

_____

_____

4. What did Joshua remind them to do when they arrived to their homes in Transjordan? (22:5)

_____

5. What did Joshua do when he sent them away? (22:6-7)

_____

What do you think this might have meant to them?

_____

_____

The Problem Altar: Joshua 22:10-34

1. What problem occurred when the Transjordan tribes went home? (22:10-12)

_____

2. How did the other tribes interpret this act? (22:12, 16)

_____

_____

3. Because of their interpretation of this action, what were the rest of the tribes driven to do? (22:12)

_____

_____

4. Before hostilities could begin, what steps did Israel take to handle this problem? (22:13-16)

    a. 22:13-14 _____

    b. 22:15-16 _____

5. What were the leaders afraid would happen because of this act? (22:15-20)

_____

_____

_____

6.   What was the explanation offered by the Transjordan tribes? (22:21-29)

_____

_____

_____

7.   How did the rest of Israel receive their explanation? (22:30-33)

_____

_____

_____

8.   What did the Reuvenites call their altar? (22:34)

_____

Why do you think they called it by that name?

_____

_____

9.   In the end, summarize what the real issues were that made for the whole conflict.

_____

_____

_____

_____

10. What are some things we can learn here about how to handle both interpersonal and corporate difficulties or conflicts?

_____

_____

_____

_____

_____

_____

Lessons from the Altar

The Altar story can provide several lessons for us all. It is

- An example of Israel's faithfulness to the Lord,
- An example of following Torah to investigate all matters thoroughly before acting,
- An example of the zealousness of all parties for the Lord, and
- An example of the unity of the Nation,

    — A very rare time in Israel's history!!

The Farewell Speech: Joshua Chapter 23

1. There are a few statements about Joshua's age in the *Book of Joshua*. We explored one of them in 13:1. Here, in 23:1 is a similar statement. What is similar and what is different about these two accounts of Joshua's age?

    _____

    _____

    _____

    _____

    _____

2. In 23:1-5 Joshua reminds Israel of some of the things He did for them. What things does Joshua list?

    _____

    _____

    _____

    _____

    _____

3. Next, in his speech, Joshua reminds Israel to:

    c. 23:6 _____

    d. 23:7 _____

    e. 23:8 _____

4. The basis for Israel being faithful to the covenant is expressed in 23:9-10. What is that basis?

    _____

    _____

    _____

5. In 23:8 and 12, the English translations use the same word to describe the kind of relationship Israel was/is to have with the Lord. What is that word?

    _____

    This word is also used in Genesis 2:24 to speak of the relationship between a husband and a wife. The Hebrew term is from the word, *davak* (דבק). In modern Hebrew it is a common term for glue. In this light, how does the wording in 23:12 help us to understand the use of this term?

    _____

    _____

    _____

    Finally, what does this word teach us about how the Lord wants us to relate to Him?

    _____

    _____

    _____

6. What did Joshua say he is now doing in 23:14-16?

    _____

    _____

7. In his final speech to the Israelites, what was foremost on Joshua's mind?

    _____

    _____

One More Time at Shechem: Joshua 24:1-28

1. Where did Joshua lead Israel for a second time?

    _____

2. What was the reason why they went there?

    _____

3. Why did he and Israel go to that specific location and not to a different location?

    _____

    _____

4. In this event, after gathering the people, what did Joshua do first? (24:1-13) _

    What purpose did this serve? _____

    _____

5. What are the key events and people which Joshua brought up in this historical summary?

    _____

    _____

    _____

    What role did each play in the history of Israel?

    _____

    _____

    _____

    _____

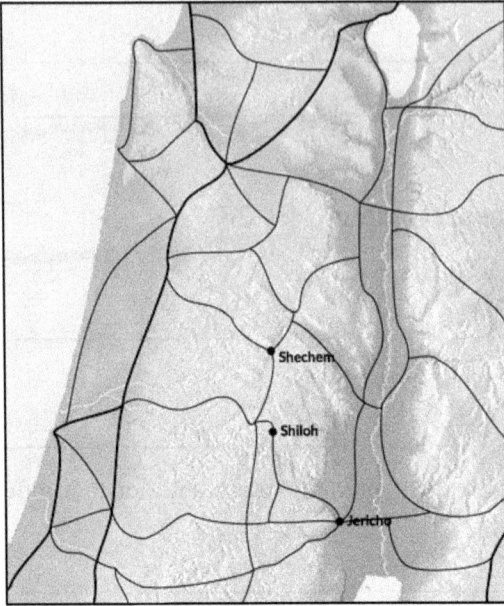

Notice the location of Shechem, especially in relation to Shiloh and Jericho.

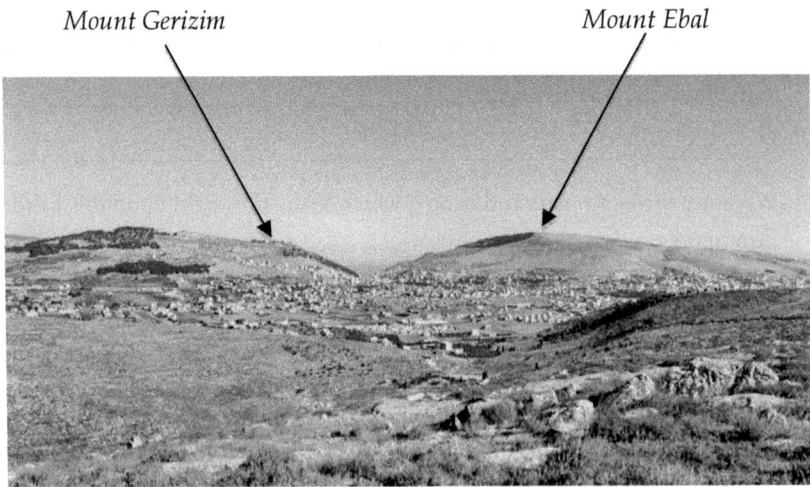

Mount Gerizim   Mount Ebal

6. According to 24:10-13, what was God's role in delivering the inhabitants of Canaan into Israel's hands?

_____

_____

7. What does 24:14 say about the forefathers of the Israelites?

   _____

   _____

   Note: The reference to "The River" is a reference to the Euphrates River.

8. The famous singer, Bob Dylan, once wrote a song in which he said, "Gotta serve somebody." Do you think that is true? _____

   Joshua 24:15 also seems to imply that we all must serve someone. What are the choices presented to the Israelites?

   _____

   _____

   What choices do we have?

   _____

   _____

   _____

9. What do you think Joshua meant in 24:15 when he said, "but me and my house shall serve the Lord?"

   _____

   _____

   What would that mean for you and your house?

   _____

   _____

   _____

10. What reason(s) did the Israelites give that caused them to want to serve the Lord? (24:16-18)

   _____

   _____

   _____

   _____

11. What did Joshua warn the people about in 24:19-20? Why did he say this to them?

_____

_____

12. What was part of their being faithful to the Holy One according to 24:24?

_____

_____

Note: When the text uses the word "obey" in this and in other places where the term is used, it reflects the Hebrew word *shema* (שמע), which means "to hear." What is the difference between "obeying" and "hearing?"

_____

_____

Why do you think the Bible uses the word "to hear" instead of "to obey?"

_____

_____

_____

13. What did Joshua do for the people after they agreed to accept the covenant renewal? (24:25-27)

_____

_____

Why were those things so important?

_____

_____

_____

Memory Verses

Joshua 24:14-15 – "Now, therefore, continually fear the Lord and serve Him continually with blamelessness and with truth; and remove the gods which your fathers served beyond the River and in Egypt, and serve the Lord...But as for me and my house, we will serve the Lord continually."

The Passing of Joshua: Joshua 24:29-33

1.   How old was Joshua when he died? _____

2.   Where was he buried? _____

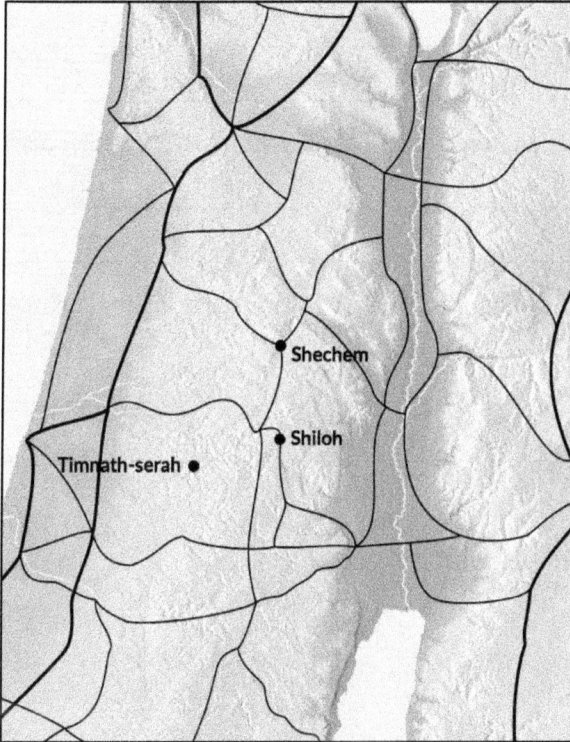

The location of Joshua's burial place at
Timnat-serah — in the heart of the Land of Israel.

3.   How was Joshua referred to after he died? (24:29)

_____

Who else was referred to in the same way after he died?

_____

4. What are some parallel's you can find between Moshe's passing, including his final sermons, with the Israelites and Joshua's passing, including his final sermons?

_____

_____

_____

5. What is the significance of mentioning the burial of Joseph's remains?

_____

_____

Note: The mention of Joseph's bones merely means his remains; he was embalmed in Egypt!

6. Why is 24:31 so historically significant?

_____

_____

_____

Memory Verse

Joshua 24:31 – "Israel served the Lord all the days of Joshua and all the days of the elders who prolonged their days after Joshua, and had known all the deeds of the Lord which He had done for Israel."

BIBLIOGRAPHY

Aharoni, Yohanan. *The Land of the Bible: A Historical Geography*. Philadelphia: Westminster Press, 1979.

Boice, James Montgomery. *Boice Expositional Commentary: Joshua*. Grand Rapids: Baker Academic, 2005.

Fishbane, Michael. *The JPS Bible Commentary: Haftarot*. Philadelphia: The Jewish Publication Society, 2002.

Frendo, Anthony J. "Was Rahab Really a Harlot?" *Biblical Archaeology Review*, September/October 2013.

Hansen, David G. "Gibeon: Its Archaeological, Geographical, and Contextual Significance." *Bible and Spade*, Winter 2007.

Harrison, R. K. *Introduction to the Old Testament*. Grand Rapids: Eerdmans, 1969.

Herzog, Chaom and Gichon, Mordechai. *Battles of the Bible*. Toronto: Stoddart Publishing, Co. Ltd., 1997.

Hess, Richard S. *Joshua (Tyndale O. T. Commentary*, Donald J. Wiseman, Gen. Ed.). Nottingham: Inter-Varsity Press, 1996.

Jones, Cambria. "Contested Conflagration: Joshua and the Conquest of Hazor." *Bible and Spade* 24.3: 79-84, 2011.

Livingston, David. "Location of Biblical Bethel and Ai Reconsidered." *Bible and Spade*. 25 June 2009.

Madvig, Donald H. *Joshua (Expositor's Bible Commentary*, Frank E. Gaebelein, Ed.). Grand Rapids: Zondervan, 1990.

Merrill, Eugene H. *Kingdom of Priests: A History of Old Testament Israel*. Grand Rapids: Baker, 1996.

— "Ai and Old Testament Chronology: Who Cares?" *Bible and Spade*, Spring 2014.

Petrovich, Doug. "The Dating of Hazor's Destruction in Joshua 11 by Way of Biblical, Archaeological, and Epigraphical Evidence." *Journal of the Evangelical Theological Society* 51.3: 489-512, 2008.

Rainey, Anson and Notley, R. Stephen. *The Sacred Bridge.* Carta: Jerusalem, 2006.

Rosenbaum, M. and Silberman, A. M., translators and annotators. *Pentateuch with Targum Onkelos, Haphtaroth, and Rashi's Commentary: Deuteronomy.* New York: Hebrew Publishing Co., N/D.

Schaeffer, Francis. *Joshua and the Flow of Biblical History.* London: Hodder and Stoughton, 1975.

Schlegel, William. *Satellite Bible Atlas: Historical Geography of the Bible*, 2012.

Smith, Henry B. "Joshua's Lost Conquest." *Bible and Spade.* Fall, 2014.

Tigay, Jeffrey H. *The JPS Torah Commentary: Deuteronomy.* Philadelphia: The Jewish Publication Society, 1996.

Walton, John H.; Matthews, Victor H.; and Chavalas, Mark W. *IVP Bible Background Commentary: Old Testament.* Downers Grove, IL: InterVarsity Press, 2000.

Wood, Bryant G. "Did the Israelites Conquer Jericho? A New Look at the Archaeological Evidence". *Bible and Spade*, 1 May 2008.

— "The Walls of Jericho." *Bible and Spade,* 9 June 2008.

Helpful Websites

www.biblearchaeology.org/
A website of the Associates for Biblical Research, an excellent source for information about archaeology from an evangelical point of view.

www.biblicalarchaeology.org/
This is the home of the popular magazine called Biblical Archaeology Review.

www.BiblePlaces.com
An important source for pictures of biblical sites and culture, both in Israel and in the Mediterranean world in general.

www.TorahResource.com

www.TorahResourcesInternational.com

www.shoreshimtri.com

Books by Ariel & D'vorah Berkowitz

Other works by the author and his wife, Ariel & D'vorah Berkowitz, include:

- *A Week in the Life of the Lamb*
- *Briteinu: A Messianic Commentary on the Weekly Torah Portions*
- *Foundations Rediscovered*
- *Hanukkah in the Home of the Redeemed*
- *How to Study and Teach the Bible*
- *Take Hold*
- *Torah Rediscovered*

To order your copy of these books, please see the website of Shoreshim Publishing (www.shoreshimtri.com)

www.ingramcontent.com/pod-product-compliance
Lightning Source LLC
Chambersburg PA
CBHW060344050426
42449CB00011B/2830